Sacagawea

A Photo-Illustrated Biography

by Barbara Witteman

Consultant:
Gerald Newborg
State Archivist
State Historical Society of North Dakota

Bridgestone Books
an imprint of Capstone Press
Mankato, Minnesota

Bridgestone Books are published by Capstone Press
151 Good Counsel Drive, P.O. Box 669, Mankato, Minnesota 56002
http://www.capstone-press.com

Library of Congress Cataloging-in-Publication Data
Witteman, Barbara.
  Sacagawea: a photo-illustrated biography/by Barbara Witteman.
  p. cm.—(Photo-illustrated biographies)
  Includes bibliographical references and index.
  Summary: A biography of the American Indian woman who served as an interpreter
on the Lewis and Clark Expedition.
  ISBN 0-7368-1112-5
  1. Sacagawea, 1786–1884—Juvenile literature. 2. Sacagawea, 1786–1884—Pictorial
works—Juvenile literature. 3. Shoshoni women—Biography—Juvenile literature.
4. Shoshoni Indians—Biography—Juvenile literature. 5. Lewis and Clark Expedition
(1804–1806)—Juvenile literature. [1. Sacagawea, 1786–1884. 2. Shoshoni Indians—
Biography. 3. Indians of North America—Biography. 4. Women—Biography. 5. Lewis
and Clark Expedition (1804–1806)] I. Title. II. Series.
F592.7.S123 W57 2002
978'.0049745—dc21   2001005405

Editorial Credits
Gillia Olson, editor; Karen Risch, product planning editor; Timothy Halldin, cover
    designer; Steve Christensen, interior layout designer; Alta Schaffer, photo researcher

Photo Credits
The Denver Public Library, Western History Collection, 4
Gary Bubbers, cover, 8, 18
Hulton/Archive Photos, 14
Jefferson National Expansion Memorial/National Park Service, 16
Marian Anderson, 10
Marilyn "Angel" Wynn, 6
North Wind Picture Archives, 12
Reuters/Blake Sell/Archive Photos, 20

The author wishes to acknowledge her parents Jack and Betty Steinberger, with love
and thanks.

1 2 3 4 5 6 07 06 05 04 03 02

Table of Contents

A Mystery

Sacagawea (suh-kah-guh-WEE-ah) is one of the most famous American Indian women who ever lived. She helped Meriwether Lewis and William Clark during their exploration of the Louisiana Territory. She helped find food. She also helped Lewis and Clark trade with the Shoshone people.

Most of Sacagawea's life is a mystery. Early American Indians did not write things down. They told stories about important events. Only a few people wrote about Sacagawea.

People disagree on the spelling of Sacagawea's name. Her name means "bird woman" in the Hidatsa language. Most people use the spelling Sacagawea. Others use Sakakawea (suh-kah-kah-WEE-ah). Both of these spellings are English spellings of the Hidatsa language. Some people use the spelling Sacajawea (sak-uh-juh-WEE-ah). This spelling changes the meaning of her name to "boat launcher."

No one drew pictures of Sacagawea while she was alive. E.S. Paxson drew this picture of what she may have looked like.

The Shoshone

Sacagawea's actual birthdate is not known. She may have been born in 1788. She was Shoshone. The Shoshone lived in the northwestern United States. This area includes the present-day states of Idaho, Wyoming, and Montana. Sacagawea's tribe lived in the Rocky Mountains.

The Shoshone moved to where they could find plants or animals to eat. The Shoshone ate the roots of the blue camas lily in the spring. During summer, they ate fish. Sacagawea's tribe went hungry when they could not find enough food.

During fall, the Shoshone went east to hunting grounds in Montana. The Shoshone had large herds of horses. They rode the horses and used bows and arrows to hunt buffalo.

The Shoshone lived in tepees. These tents were easy to take down, move, and rebuild.

Captured

In 1800, the Shoshone fought a battle with the Hidatsa near Three Forks, Montana. The Hidatsa had guns. The Shoshone had only bows and arrows. The Hidatsa easily defeated the Shoshone.

Sacagawea was about 12 years old. She and other Shoshone children were captured and taken to the Hidatsa village. This village was on the Knife River in North Dakota. It was about 500 miles (800 kilometers) from Sacagawea's mountain home. The Mandan Indians lived near the Hidatsa.

The Hidatsa lived in earth houses. These houses were called earth lodges. They had large gardens. They grew enough vegetables to last all year. They also hunted wild animals.

Sacagawea worked with the women. She learned how to plant and harvest crops. Sacagawea had to work very hard. She learned a new way of life. She became a member of the Hidatsa tribe.

The Hidatsa lived in earth lodges. This re-creation is located at On-A-Slant village in North Dakota.

The Expedition

Sacagawea met her husband Toussaint (too-SAHNT) Charbonneau (SHAR-buh-noh) a few years after her capture. Charbonneau was a French fur trader. He had lived with the Mandan and Hidatsa for a long time. Charbonneau could speak different languages. He was about 25 years older than Sacagawea.

On October 26, 1804, the Lewis and Clark expedition arrived at the Mandan-Hidatsa villages. Lewis and Clark were leading an exploration of the Louisiana Territory. The United States had bought this huge area of land west of the Mississippi River.

Lewis and Clark needed interpreters. They wanted to know what the American Indians they met were saying. They hired Charbonneau. Lewis and Clark also needed a person who spoke Shoshone. They agreed to let Sacagawea come with them because she spoke Shoshone.

Marian Anderson painted this picture of Sacagawea as she may have appeared during the expedition.

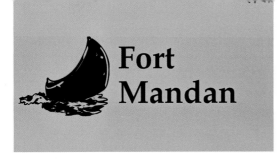

Fort Mandan

The expedition could not leave right away. They needed a place to live during winter. The men built Fort Mandan.

On February 11, 1805, Sacagawea gave birth to her son, Jean (ZHAN) Baptiste (bap-TEEST). Sacagawea was about 16 years old. Clark gave the boy the nickname "Pomp."

The expedition headed west on April 7, 1805. First, they had to find where the Missouri River began. Next, they had to find a way through the Rocky Mountains. Finally, they hoped to float down the Columbia River to the Pacific Ocean. The men in the expedition made careful records of what they saw. Lewis, Clark, and three other men kept journals. They wrote about the things that they saw. They also wrote about Sacagawea.

Members of the expedition built Fort Mandan to live in during the winter of 1804–1805. This reconstruction shows how Fort Mandan looked.

"The wife of Shabono [Charbonneau] our interpreter...is a token of peace."
–William Clark, writing about Sacagawea, journal entry, October 13, 1805

Sacagawea's Help

Sacagawea helped the expedition in many ways. She helped them find food. She knew where animals would bury dried roots and seeds. She found wild beans and artichokes that animals had stored. Sacagawea dug wild licorice root, white apple roots, onions, and other roots. She also picked wild fruit.

Sacagawea was most important to the expedition because she was a woman. American Indians knew the group was peaceful when they saw Sacagawea. A woman would not travel with a war party.

Sacagawea did not guide the group. But she did recognize some features on the land. She told the men when they were getting close to the Three Forks. This area was the starting point of the Missouri River. She also showed them the Bozeman Pass in the Rocky Mountains. This gap made it easier to cross the mountains than other trails.

Sacagawea was important to the expedition because she showed that the group was peaceful.

Meeting the Shoshone

About midway through the journey, Lewis and Clark planned to find the Shoshone. The Shoshone had many horses. The group needed horses to get through the mountains. Lewis and Clark wanted Sacagawea to help them trade with the Shoshone.

They finally met the Shoshone in August 1805. Lewis and Clark sent for Sacagawea. Sacagawea recognized the Shoshone chief. It was her brother, Cameahwait (kah-MEE-ah-wayt). They were happy to see each other again.

Sacagawea helped Lewis and Clark trade for horses. Expedition members brought trade goods to exchange for things they needed. Some trade goods were silk handkerchiefs, ribbons, mirrors, and beads. The expedition members traded some of these goods for horses.

After a hard trip, the group reached the Pacific coast in November. They spent the winter there.

Lewis and Clark met the Shoshone in August 1805.

"Your woman who accompanied you that long dangerous and fatiguing rout to the Pacific Ocian and back diserved a greater reward for her attention and services on that rout than we had in our power to give her."
–William Clark, in a letter to Charbonneau, August 20, 1806

Journey's End

On March 23, 1806, the group headed home. They reached the Knife River in mid-August. The men said good-bye to Sacagawea and her family. Charbonneau received $500.33 for his services. Sacagawea received no pay.

Clark offered to take Pomp to St. Louis with him. He would treat Pomp as if he were his son. Charbonneau and Sacagawea agreed. Pomp would live with Clark after he grew older.

Little was written about Sacagawea after the trip ended. She and Charbonneau visited Clark in St. Louis in 1809. Sacagawea and Charbonneau then returned to their home on the Knife River.

In 1812, Charbonneau worked as a fur trader at Fort Manuel (MAN-yoo-uhl). This fort was on the Missouri River. Sacagawea gave birth to her daughter, Lizette, at the fort in August.

This statue in Bismarck, North Dakota, was created about 100 years after the expedition ended.

Lasting Mystery

People disagree about when Sacagawea died. On December 20, 1812, a clerk at Fort Manuel wrote that the wife of Charbonneau had died of a fever. In 1813, Sacagawea's children went to live with Clark. He took care of them.

Some Shoshone believe that Sacagawea died in Wyoming on April 9, 1884. She would have been nearly 100 years old. Many non-Shoshone historians do not believe this story.

People have honored Sacagawea in many ways. Three mountains, 23 monuments, and two lakes are named after her. In 2000, the U.S. government made a coin with her image on it. North Dakota will place a statue of Sacagawea and Pomp in Statuary Hall in Washington, D.C. This room holds two statues from each of the 50 states.

Randy'l Hedow Teton was the model for the Sacagawea dollar coin.

Fast Facts about Sacagawea

 Sacagawea calmly saved valuable tools and journals when her canoe tipped in the Missouri River during the expedition.

 To interpret Shoshone, Sacagawea repeated the Shoshone words to her husband in Hidatsa. Charbonneau then spoke in French to another man. This man interpreted the French to English.

 Clark named a river in Montana after Sacagawea. He called it Sacagawea's River or Bird Woman's River.

Dates in Sacagawea's Life

1788?—Sacagawea is born in present-day Idaho.

1800—Sacagawea is captured by the Hidatsa, near Three Forks, Montana.

1804—The Lewis and Clark Expedition arrives at the Knife River villages on October 26.

1805—Jean Baptiste is born at Fort Mandan on February 11.
The Lewis and Clark Expedition leaves Fort Mandan on April 7.
Sacagawea meets with the Shoshone on August 13.

1806—Sacagawea and her family leave the expedition at Fort Mandan on August 17.

1809–1811—Sacagawea and Charbonneau visit Clark in St. Louis.

1812—Sacagawea gives birth to Lizette at Fort Manuel in August.
Sacagawea dies at Fort Manuel on December 20.

Words to Know

artichoke (AR-ti-choke)—a thistlelike plant; people can eat the flower.

blue camas lily (BLOO KAM-us LIL-ee)—a plant that grows from a bulb and has stalks of small, blue flowers

clerk (KLURK)—a person who keeps written records

expedition (ek-spuh-DISH-uhn)—a long journey for a certain purpose, such as exploring

exploration (ek-spluh-RAY-shuhn)—the act of traveling to discover what a place is like

interpreter (in-TUR-prit-uhr)—someone who can tell others what is said in another language

journal (JUR-nuhl)—a diary in which people regularly write down their thoughts and experiences

pass (PASS)—a gap between mountains

Read More

Mattern, Joanne. *The Shoshone People.* Native Peoples. Mankato, Minn.: Bridgestone Books, 2001.

Morley, Jacqueline. *Across America: The Story of Lewis & Clark.* Expedition. New York: Franklin Watts, 1998.

Thomasma, Kenneth. *The Truth about Sacajawea.* Jackson, Wyo.: Grandview Publishing, 1997.

Useful Addresses

The Lewis and Clark Trail Heritage Foundation, Inc.
P.O. Box 3434
Great Falls, MT 59403

North Dakota Lewis and Clark Interpretive Center
P.O. Box 607
Washburn, ND 58577-0607

Internet Sites

History Commentary—The Sacagawea Mystique
http://www.wshs.org/columbia/0399-a1.htm
Lewis and Clark in North Dakota
http://www.fortmandan.org
State Historical Society of North Dakota: Sakakawea
http://www.state.nd.us/hist/sakakawea.htm

Index